W9-BTT-133

the Louvre

the Louvre

Text by

Michel Gallet
attaché à la Conservation
du Musée Carnavalet

f. hazan éditeur
EXCLUSIVITÉ VILO
5 RUE DE SAVOIE PARIS 6

The Louvre.

The National Convention inaugurated the Louvre museum on the 8th November, 1793. The original idea was not theirs, because the decision to open the royal collections to the public had been taken under Louis XV and was under consideration for a long time by the administration of the Ancien Régime. The temporary opening of the Luxembourg galleries in the middle of the century had in a way anticipated the Louvre and the influence of the philosophical movement had encouraged these innovations. The long week of the revolutionary calendar allowed five days for artists' copying the pictures and two days for the public, which left three days of rest for the attendants and cleaning the rooms. The royal collections formed the basis of the present museum. Francis I welcomed Leonardo da Vinci's studio in Touraine and the same year he bought Andrea del Sarto's *Charity* from the artist. Raphael's *Holy Family* was offered to him by the Duke of Florence on behalf of Pope Leo X. Louis XIII received works of art bequeathed to him by Richelieu. Louis XIV enlarged this artistic wealth considerably by buying collections belonging to the banker, Jabach, Mazarin and Charles I of England. Several paintings of the great 16th century Venetians were acquired in this way. Veronese's *Feast at Simon's House*, now at Versailles, was a present from Venice to Louis XIV. What the Roi Soleil had not done was accomplished by the monarchy in its decline. Under Louis XVI, the Comte d'Angiviller, the Superintendant of Public Buildings, made regular purchases in anticipation of the museum's opening. He shared the tastes of art-lovers of his time for the northern schools and the Dutch paintings he gathered together are among the proudest possessions of the Louvre today. When the Revolution broke out, the selected and restored paintings waited, propped against the walls of the Grande Galerie, for a public that already knew its way to the palace; the biennials of the Royal Academy, the ''Salons '' that Diderot had discussed, used to take place in the Salon Carré.

The conquests of the Directoire, the Consulate and the Empire brought works of art flooding into the Louvre and it agreed to deposit a great many of them in provincial museums. The antiquities were placed in the galleries with walls of Pompeian stucco work, where they remain today. Napoleon, as First Consul, inaugurated them at six o'clock in the morning and invited the curators to dinner. However, after the Empire fell, France had to return what she had taken. Some paintings were kept with a certain amount of subterfuge. It was alleged that Veronese's *Wedding at Cana* was too delicate to transport. Venice received in exchange Le Brun's *Magdalen at the Feet of Christ*, which has now been relegated to the Palazzo Marcello where nobody sees it. At Caen, the Italian Commissioners were served a meal on the panel of Pinturicchio's *Marriage of the Virgin*, turned face down on the tressels. There is no counting the ungracious comments and galling observations made by Italian museum curators in front of the gaps left at Fiesole by the Fra Angelico, at Mantua by the Perugino, and Isabella d'Este's Mantegna.

New civilisations were represented in the museum under Louis-Philippe. The Egyptian section was opened in 1833, when Champollion had just solved the riddle of hieroglyphics. Botta's excavations at Khorsabad led to the opening of the Assyrian galleries. The Comte de Marcellus bought the famous Venus de Milo. Later on, the consul, Chantoiseau, brought back the *Victory of Samothrace* and the galley she adorned. The most recent acquisitions are due to the generosity of individuals. The La Caze, Thomy-Thiéry and Chauchard donations enriched the 18th century collections and introduced the Barbizon School. The impressionists collected by Moreau-Nélaton, Personnaz, Camondo and Gachet were gathered together in the Musée du Jeu de Paume. The Walter collection in the nearby Orangerie will be a marvellous complement to them.

Ancient Middle East. The oriental antiquities of the Louvre reflect an even more ancient past than Egypt's, and civilisations scattered over a vaster geographical area stretching from the Bosphorus to the Persian Gulf. The confused and often blood-stained history of the ancient Middle East was woven of the migrations, ambitions, struggles and exchanges of three groups, Asianic, Indo-European and Semitic. Excavations in Mesopotamia and Iran since the middle of the 19th century have brought new life to the millenniums on which the Bible, Greek historians and Egyptology only offer indirect evidence.

The Mesopotamian sites of Mari, Lagash (Tello) and Larsa have revealed the brilliance of the Sumero-Akkadian civilisation in the first half of the 3rd millenium B.C. The *Vulture Stele* commemorates the victory of Ennatum, king of Lagash, during a war with the neighbouring town of Umma for the possession of a plam-grove. Here, as well as on the *Stele of Naram-Sin*, the subject of the fighting king appears, which was one of the most frequently treated in the art of Mesopotamia and Egypt. The prisoners, caught in a net, are about to be clubbed to death by the god, Ningirsu; the Lagash army marches behind Ennatum's chariot, who is wielding his lance and yatagan; and the vultures are settling on the dead. Lagash reached its apogee under the rule of Gudea, whose appearance has been preserved fo us in a series of massive statues. On two of them, Gudea is depicted as an architect, measuring-rod in hand plotting the ground-plan of a temple dedicated to his protector, Ningirsu.

During the 2nd millennium B.C., the dominions of the Sumerian monarchs were still quite small and left plenty of room for the huge Mesopotamian empires of Babylon and Assyria. The stele, inscribed with King Hammurabi's code in abstract characters called cuneiform writing, promulgates the law of this Babylonian king nineteen centuries before our era. It touches on all the eventualities of private life. The principle of the lex talionis prescribed the penalties, and the exercise of the liberal professions was strictly regulated; the clumsy use of the bistoury or the collapse of a new building, a frequent occurrence during the Euphrates' floods, could lead to the death of the surgeon or architect, and even his wife and children. The end of the millennium saw the rise of the Assyrian Empire which filled all the east with the clash of arms. The main aim of its art was to

Sumerian art.
Ebi-Hil, the " Steward of Mari ".
28th century B.C.

PHOTOS GIRAUDON

Babylonian art.
Stele inscribed with King Hammurabi
code of law. 18th century B.C.

provide a magnificent setting for the lives of its emperors and
impress their subjects with an intimidating image of their power.
The huge bas-reliefs from Sargon II's palace at Khorsabad
certainly succeed in doing this. One of them illustrates the
construction of the palace, the cedars cut down in Lebanon,
transported by sea and land, and hoisted to the site by ropes.
On others we can see the tutelary demi-god, Gilgamesh,
casually crushing a lion under his arm, or Sargon's servants
bringing their master a table, a chair, a dish of food or the detach-
ed pieces from his chariot. The deportation scenes on bas-
reliefs from the royal palace of Assur-bani-pal at Nineveh seem
to correspond to the Biblical story of the captivity at Babylon.
The identity of the image with its object resulted in artistic
conventions similar to those of Egyptian art; the great *Winged
Bulls* of Khorsabad are each given five feet so that they appear
as complete from the front view as from the side.

11

Assyrian art. King Assur-bani-pal in his chariot. 8th century B.C.

Sculptures, ceramics, goldsmith's work, and seals are beauti-
fully decorated with innumerable animals depicted with an
admirable skill by these ferocious hunters: the *Man carrying a
Kid* from Khorsabad, ceramics from Susa with ibexes stylised
to the point of abstraction, an Iranian bracelet in electron with
six lions' heads, fantastic animals on bronzes from Luristan.

The Assyrian splendours of Nimrod, Nineveh and Khorsabad
were rivalled in the 1st millennium B.C. by Achaemenid Persia,
a huge empire whose vanguard clashed with the little Greek
people at Salamis. The *Capital* with two protomoi of bulls is a
relic of the apadana, or portico of Artaxerxes at Susa; it used to
support a ceiling of cedar 75 ft above the ground. The uniform
repetition of the same figure, in the *Frieze of Archers* from Susa,
along a wall of glazed brick produces an obsessive illusion of
perpetual movement.

Art of Achaemenid Persia.
Frieze of archers.   Glazed bricks.   5 th century B.C.

Egypt. At the beginning of the 3rd millennium B.C. in the
fertile valley of the Nile, there appeared the Egyptian civilisation which survived to the beginning of our own era. After
the pre-historic ages and totemism, its religion taught the survival of the soul and the divinity of the pharaoh in the life
hereafter. The indispensable condition for this survival was
the preservation of the body, so its mummy was sheltered in
an inviolable sepulchre. This was provided by innumerable
mastabas, or funerary edifices, and the pyramids, which remain
as memorials to the pharaohs of the Old Kingdom, established
at Memphis in Lower Egypt.

The visitor penetrating the mastaba of Akhut-hotep, an
important official of the Vth Dynasty, can see at a glance the
quality of Egyptian figurative art. Familiar scenes are represented on it in low, polychrome relief. It must be remembered

13

that the image was identified with its object and possessed a magic power; in the entrance corridor, the portrait of the dead man seated was his " double " which his soul returned to inhabit. Each part of the body is represented at the angle where it appeared most complete to ensure that its magical power would be most efficacious; the bust is front view, so is the eye set in a head in profile, the hips are three-quarters view, the legs side view. No figure could mask another and each of the superposed registers represents a plane at a greater or less depth. The Egyptian was a realist, who took natural forms for the characters of his writing and here he appears as a great animal artist. Fishermen spread their nets in the Nile waters swarming with fish and brave a hippopotamus threatening their embarkation; an antelope protects its little one which a wolf is about to pounce on; birds sing in the trees; servants lead oxen and donkeys, hold ducks by their feet and carry baskets of fruit, all of which are acceptable offerings to the dead man and necessary for supporting his second existence. These ideas explain the large number of familiar objects found in the tombs. There is on show at the Louvre a trigonal harp, an armchair, toilet and hair-dressing accessories which recreate for us the atmosphere of everyday life on the banks of the Nile.

The belief in a " double " and abundant supplies of stone and wood encouraged the rise of sculpture. Egyptian statuary always conformed to the law of frontality which keeps the head on the axis of the bust. It is represented in the museum by several masterpieces of Memphite realism: an *Official and his Wife; Sekhemka; King Didoufri;* the *Squatting Scribe* and the *Head of a Man*, known as the Salt Head.

The Middle Kingdom, which was a period of social evolution, saw the democratising of funerary rites, in other words, everyone had the right to an after-life. The cult of the dead and the mythology governing it were a constant stimulus for the figurative art on sarcophagus cases and funerary chambers. The animal form given to gods in the illustrations of sacred legends was probably a relic of totemism. The evil-minded Seth is a greyhound or okapi, the sun god, Horus, is a falcon and the ibis, Thot, is clerk to the celestial tribunal. The dead in their ordeals relived the passion of Osiris, who was torn to pieces by a divine conjuration. His mummy, the first of its kind, was borne by the Nile to its entombment and after his apotheosis he became the God of the Dead. A number of objects were associated with these beliefs: a statuette of

14

Egyptian art. Bearers of offerings. Polychrome bas-relief from the mastaba of Akhut-Hetep. Vth Dynasty. About 2400 B.C.

Osiris, a hymn and a tabernacle dedicated to the god, the Book of the Dead which was a collection of magic formulas useful to the traveller in the after-life (the *coffin of the chancellor, Nakhti*). Thebes in Upper Egypt was the capital of the New Kingdom, which was distinguished by the conquest of the Rameses pharaohs. Statuary had developed from the realism of the Old Kingdom towards idealisation, but it still retained a sensitive conception of feminine grace. The forms of the *Woman carrying a Trough*, the *Lady Tui* who was the superior of a community of recluses, and the cat-headed *Goddess Bastet* are delicately moulded by the sheath of their long, clinging dresses. A hair style with a fringe was the favourite of elegant or athletic women, like the swimmer who forms the handle of cosmetic spoons. During the New Kingdom, the monotheistic heresy of Amenophis IV (Akhnaton), husband of the beautiful Asiatic, Nefertiti, led to the renaissance of a powerful naturalism which was sometimes taken to the point of caricature. The pharaoh is portrayed in the museum by a bust and the royal couple in a bas-relief. In the 1st millennium B.C., Saitic art deteriorated through its contact with eastern peoples. The original character of Egyptian art was later on weakened by Greek influence and finally succumbed under Roman domination in spite of the conquerors' respect for its ancient traditions.

15

Egyptian art.
Queen Karomama.
Bronze inlaid with gold.
XXIInd Dynasty.   About 850 B.C.

PHOTO ALINARI-GIRAUDON

Egyptian art.   The Squatting Scribe.
Vth Dynasty.   About 2400 B.C.

PHOTO   GIRAUDON

Greece and Rome. Every European admires in Greek sculpture the most accomplished of all representations of the human figure; it is an art that he naturally associates with the idea of perfection. The Greek religion rejected the hybrid and monstrous divinities that terrified the imagination of orientals and the predecessors of the Hellenes. In remote times, as far back as the memory of the Greeks could take them, Oedipus had destroyed the sphinx; the age of mystery and terror was followed by the age of clear intelligence and concepts forged by the human mind; dark beliefs were transformed into myth. The gods took on the physical appearance of men, and perso-

16

ART EGYPTIEN. LA « PORTEUSE D'AUGE ». XIᵉ-XIIᵉ DYNASTIE
EGYPTIAN ART. WOMAN CARRYING A TROUGH. XIth-XIIth DYNASTY
ÄGYPTISCHE KUNST. DIE « TROGTRÄGERIN ». XI-XII DYNASTIE
ARTE EGIPCIO. « MUJER LLEVANDO UNA ARTESA ». XIº-XIIº DINASTIA
ARTE EGIZIANA. LA « PORTATRICE DI VASCHETTA ». XIº-XIIº DINASTIA

Egyptian art.
Head of a man, called the Salt Head.
IVth-Vth Dynasty   About 2425 B.C.

PHOTO VIGNEAU

Greek art.
Head of a man, called the " Rampin Horseman ".
About 560-550 B.C.

PHOTO TEL

nified their faculties and passions. They considered the spec-
tacle of nude athletes in action the most flattering of offerings
and this created an inexhaustible source for sculpture at the
end of the 7th century B.C.

The primitive *Venus of Auxerre*, which was probably analo-
gous to the old wooden idols or xoana, is the incunabulum of
Greek sculpture. In the 6th century B.C., the archaic period
gradually perfected the two types of the kouros, the athlete or
Apollo, and the young, clothed woman, or kore. Two distinct
temperaments divided the Greek people at that time and were
equally reflected in its art. Energy, the warrior virtues and
seriousness characterised the Dorians of mainland Greece and
the Peloponnesus. Ionia, the coast region of Asia Minor, introduced the feminine elegance, the smile and voluptuousness of

17

Greek art.   The Ergastinai in the Panathenaea procession.
From the frieze on the Parthenon at Athens.   447-432 B.C.

the east. The *Hera of Samos* represents a marvellous stage in
the progress of archaic art towards the discovery of its feminine
ideal; the sensitive curves of the modelling harmonise with the
austerely carved, oblique and vertical folds of the chiton and
himation, in rather light materials, worn by Ionian women. The
kouros type is represented by the *Apollo of Actium* and the

Greek art.
Ariadne.
Detail from a Roman
copy.
About 200 B.C.

Greek art.
The Victory
of Samothrace.
About 200 B.C.

Apollo of Paros; the frontal attitude, the arms hardly lifted away
from the body and left leg stretched in front, all indicate the
persistence of an influence from Egypt, where the port of Nau-
cratis attracted Greek trade. In the second half of the 6th century, Ionian influence was preponderant in Greek civilisation and
spread over Attica. A faint smile lights the face of the *Rampin
Horseman* found at Athens. After 500 B.C., the eclipse of
Ionia, invaded by the Persians, was compensated by the vitality
of mainland Greece. The use of sculpture to decorate temples
accustomed artists to composition in high and low relief within
the architectural framework of the frieze and triangular tym-
panum of the pediment. The narrower, square area of the

19

PHOTO TEL

Greek art.
Venus of Vienne.
Roman copy.
About 200 B.C.

Greek art.
Torso of Aphrodite.
Roman copy.

metope only offered space for two or three actors in a brief episode: *Herakles taming the Cretan Bull* and *Herakles offering Athena the Stymphalian Birds* refer to two exploits of the demi-god dear to the Dorian ideal.

Victory in the Persian Wars, followed by a few years of peace within the city and security abroad saw the brief but brilliant apogee of Athenian civilisation under Pericles. Greek classicism flowered beneath the chisel of Phidias and his followers, who worked together on the Parthenon. The *Frieze of the Pana-thenaea Procession*, bearing Athena the veil woven for her every four years, ran round the cella of the temple. Solemnity and naturalness, a musical rhythm and the spirituality of a master, who had been initiated into the Eleusinian mysteries

20

are united in this beautiful work. The Louvre is not so lucky as the British Museum and only possesses a short sequence of the Panathenaea, the *Ergastinai*, the noble young women who had shared the making of the veil. The three heads known as the Laborde, La Coulonche and Humphrey-Ward Heads, are in the same style as the Parthenon art. Phidias was the centre of a group of sculptors, representing Athenian classicism, who are better known by antique replicas in marble than by their bronze originals which were melted down. The feminine nude, as represented by the *Esquiline Venus*, is still remarkable. Polycletus of Argos modelled the musculature of his *Diadumenos* with great simplicity and established the canon of masculine proportions. Like Naucydes in his *Discophoros*, he posed the athlete in a relaxed attitude in contrast to Myron's *Discobolos* in the Vatican which had astonished with its swift movement. Although mainland Greece was shaken by the Peloponnesian War, its sculpture remained supreme in the 4th century B.C. The work of Lysippus of Sycion is characterised by its unstable postures like that of *Hermes tying his*

Etruscan art. Sarcophagus in painted terra-cotta. 6th century B.C.

Sandal and he modified Polycletus's canon by reducing the head, which new measured one eighth of the body. But the decadence of Athens made her abandon Athena for Aphrodite. The courtesan, Phryne, inspired in Praxiteles the type of Venus, which was popularised in the Roman period, like those of Scopas with their excessively affected modesty. With a newly acquired knowledge of feminine anatomy, sculptors narrowed the shoulders and curved the waist over rounded hips. The *Venus of Cnidos* is a better example of Praxiteles' art than the *Venus of Arles*, because a sacrilegious chisel pared the face and breast of the goddess in an aesthetic operation performed under Louis XIV.

Alexander's conquests spread Hellenism over the greater part of the Mediterranean world. The destruction of cities and local cults hastened the decline of traditional beliefs and encouraged the mystical religions of the east that promised immortality to their initiates. The moral climate and individualism they fostered, far from provoking the decline of Greek art, stimulated

Burgundian art Tomb óf Philippe Pot
by Antoine Le Moiturier. Painted stone. Late 15th century.

PHOTOS GIRAUDON

Florentine art.
Bust of a woman.
Painted wood. 15th century

German art.
St Magdalen by Gregor Erhart.
Painted wood. Early 16th century.

it to new conceptions that were vital with grace and humour, realism and emotion. Agasia of Ephesus sculpted a Gladiator where the musculature and venous system is analysed in minute detail. One after another the sculptors discovered new modes of expression in children's games (*Boy with a Goose*), the unappeased anguish of *Ariadne Sleeping*, the tortured cries of *Marsyas*, the deformity of the *Rachitic Man*. New forms of beauty, like the eternal youth of the *Three Graces*, have been described as Alexandrian. Doidalsas' *Venus*, of which the museum possesses three examples, is the study of a mortal

woman after her bath. Attached to the back of a statue in a fine
Roman copy (*Venus of Vienne*), there remains the small hand
of a child whose body has disappeared; Eros was rubbing his
mother's back. Two of the most famous sculptures in the
Louvre belong to this period, the *Venus de Milo* and the *Victory
of Samothrace*. No replica of the first, which may be an Amphi-
trite, exists today to show us the position of the broken arms.
The mutilated hand of the Victory was found in 1950. Standing
on the prow of the galley, which has been restored, her draperies whipped by the seawind, she used to make a gesture of
greeting.

After the Roman victory at Pydna, subjugated Greece, as
Horace remarked, conquered her ferocious vanquishers. Rome
assimilated the Hellenic ideal, invited Greek artists to Italy and
imitated the masterpieces of a sculpture that we should know
inadequately without its copies. Only the architecture of the Romans is a proof of the organising genius of the conquerors. However, the age of Augustus brought new life to the art of bas-relief
as an illustration of civic virtues (*Sacrifices of a sow, a sheep or a
bull*). The Louvre also possesses a fragment of the *Ara Pacis*
(Altar of Peace), a glorification of Augustus's family which a
fictitious genealogy connected with the descendants of Trojan
Aeneas. The neo-classicism of the work is a reflection of the
Parthenon art, but the austere groups express more strongly
than Athens the social hierarchy and cohesion of the family.
From Augustus to the Antonines and Severi, Roman realism
stamped a striking individuality on the imperial busts and statues
of women, which can be dated by the curious variations in
hair styles (*Octavius as an Orator, Agrippa, Octavia, Julia
Domna, Julia Mamaea, Julia Paula*).

Sculpture. At the moment, medieval and modern sculpture
is not as well represented in the Louvre as painting. The first
sculptures in the museum came from the destruction of a great
many buildings in France during the Revolution and Empire.
Paintings share the fate of other movable furnishings, but
nearly all the masterpieces of sculptures were intended for
the permanent adornment of a building. While admiring them,
we often have to remember the churches, châteaux and abbeys
of pre-revolutionary France from where many of them have
come. In Paris, the churches of the Celestines, Dominicans,
Augustinians and Jesuits were once museums of funerary
sculpture, as the Basilique de Saint-Denis or the Santa Croce

Michelangelo. 1475-1564. Slaves intended for the tomb of Pope Julius II. Executed between 1513 and 1520.

at Florence and San Zanipolo at Venice are still. The statue of the dead man, lying on his tomb, with hands joined in prayer for all eternity, was a type of sculpture originating in the Middle Ages (*Tomb of Louis de Poncher* and *Robert Legendre* by Guillaume Regnault). Sometimes the figures placed in niches along the outside of the tomb are mourners that hold his shield. In the Louvre, the mourners of *Philippe Pot*, the great Seneschal of Burgundy, bear the recumbent figure on their shoulders. The naturalism of the Renaissance sometimes went as far as showing the dead man lying naked and in a state of decomposition (*Valente Balbiani* by Germain Pilon). The 16th century and the neo-classical period preferred the statue of the dead kneeling in prayer: *Amiral Philippe Chabot* by Bontemps; *Marie de Brabançon*, wife of the historian, De Thou, by Barthélemy Prieur. The most graceful sculptures of the Middle Ages were statues of the Virgin Mary where the slight inflexion of the torso compensated for the weight of the Child carried by the mother on her left arm (*Virgins* of Ouville la Bien Tournée, Maisoncelles, Cîteaux and Olivet). Germain Pilon had the audacity to introduce the *Three Graces* in the Greco-Roman tradition on the funerary monument of Henri II's heart, sculpted for the Église des Célestins. French 16th century sculpture possessed in Jean Goujon the great master whom the School of Fontainebleau lacked (*Nymphs and Tritons* from the Fontaine des Innocents; *Jube* from Saint Germain l'Auxerrois). *Diana with a Deer*, sculpted for Diane de Poitiers for her château at Anet, was attributed to him for a long time. The elongated lines of the goddess's body resemble Primaticcio's caryatids at Fontainebleau; sculpture has rarely modelled the human body with such ornamental suppleness. Italy, where this style originated, is represented by Agostino di Duccio, the Botticelli of sculpture (*Virgin of Auvillers*), and chance has brought here two of Michelangelo's *Slaves*, intended for the tomb of Julius II. These relics of an over-ambitious project belonged first to Henri II, then to the Montmorency and Richelieu families. With all the power in their muscles, they are straining to break the bonds of their servitude and, as a symbol of the spiritual life for those who believe in it, they express the anguish of the soul in its difficult ascent to blessedness. They are not completely disengaged from the marble and gradine marks still remain on the rough surface. The figures are charged with such intense emotion that, when he saw them at Richelieu's château, La Fontaine wrote: " What they lack makes the workman as great as all the perfection he has given them. " This unfinished effect takes on a dramatic significance in Michelangelo's last Pietà. Puget's *Milo of Croton* in the 17th century is an equally fine expression of captive power, as the man, with his hand imprisoned in the crevice of an oak tree, is mauled by a lion. When the crate, in which it was packed at Toulon, was opened at Versailles, Le Brun had the honesty to praise its qualities before Louis XIV, but the misanthropic and unhappy sculptor never found favour with the king. The Louvre used to exhibit a work

Antoine Coysevox. 1640-1720.
Bust of Louis de Bourbon,
Prince of Condé. 1688.

Jean-Antoine Houdon. 1741-1828.
Bust of Louise Brongniart as a child. 1777.

more in conformity with the ideal of elegant majesty cherished by the Roi Soleil and his court. This is Mazarin's marble tomb by Coysevox and Tuby, which has now crossed the Seine and been returned to its place in the chapel of the Institut. Now that the Pavillon de Flore has been recovered from the Ministère des Finances, the extensive exhibition area will certainly give a generous amount of space to those graceful masters, Adam, Houdon, Pajou, Falconet whose work maintained a leading place for French sculpture in the 18th century.

Cimabue.   1240?-1302?.
The Madonna of the Angels.

PHOTO S GIRAUDON

Pisanello.   1395?-1455?.
A Princess
of the House of Este.
About 1440.

Painting. The finest expression of medieval painting is in its mosaics, frescoes and stained-glass. Miniatures shared the fate of the manuscripts they illustrated and are deposited in libraries. Enamels, majolica and tapestry, those other forms of art in colour can be seen in the department of Objets d'Art in the Louvre. Panel painting also existed in classical times and the Middle Ages and they are represented in the museum by the portraits from Fayum (Antiquités Classiques) and a few Byzantine icons (Antiquités Chrétiennes). However, the economic and social changes of the 14th and 15th centuries encouraged the rise of easel painting. A refinement in the tastes of princes, the newly acquired wealth of the upper middle classes, the luxury of houses and private chapels, the rivalry of

FRA ANGELICO. 1387-1455. LE COURONNEMENT DE LA VIERGE. APRÈS 1437
FRA ANGELICO. CORONATION OF THE VIRGIN. AFTER 1437
FRA ANGELICO. DIE KRÖNUNG MARIAE. NACH 1437
FRA ANGELICO. 1387-1455. LA CORONACION DE LA VIRGEN. DESPUES DE 1437
FRA ANGELICO. 1387-1455. L'INCORONAZIONE DELLA VERGINE. DOPO 1437

Domenico Ghirlandaio
1449-1494.
An old man
and his grandson.

Antonello da Messina.
About 1430-1479.
Portrait of a man,
called the "Condottiere".

monastic communities, all fostered the birth of the picture which
is the principal pictorial expression of modern times.

Italy. Cimabue's *Madonna of the Angels* illustrates the persistence of Byzantine influence in medieval Italian painting;

29

PHOTO GIRAUDON

Alesso Baldovinetti.   1425-1499.   Virgin and Child.

the symmetry is exact, the attitudes rigid and the Madonna is larger than the angels to indicate her superior position in the celestial hierarchy. It is an art primarily concerned with the supernatural and symbolical expression of doctrinal truths. In the 13th century the preaching of St Francis of Assisi stirred a new feeling in artists towards a loving and detailed observation of nature. Giotto rejected Byzantine hierarchism, introduced realistic portraiture and suggested the drama of a situation by the movement of the figures and the facial expression of their feelings and passions (*St Francis receiving the Stigmata*). His Florentine successors (Bernardo Daddi: *Annunciation*) discovered the artistic appeal of feminine beauty and iridescent colour. The charm of Siena, which had produced some original reactions to Giotto's style, cast its spell over them. Duccio di Buoninsegna and Simone Martini (*Christ carrying the Cross*) introduced the familiar details of everyday life into the saints' legends, an unaccustomed gentleness into the faces of the Virgin and angels, and emotion into scenes of martyrdom and

Andrea Mantegna. 1431-1506. Calvary. About 1456-1459.

the Passion. Imperceptibly, the Sienese School evolved from Byzantine rigidity to the decorative, sentimental and anecdotic style of Sano di Pietro (*St Jerome and the Lion*) and Sassetta (*Virgin with St Anthony and St John the Baptist*). Their art was in keeping with an international current of naturalism, which was slightly sophisticated by the aristocratic grace of princely courts. This naturalism, which took a mystical bent in Bruges, Cologne, Westphalia, and a wolrdly one at the court of the Duc de Berry, inspired Pisanello in Italy. He was an artist of Verona, a skilful medal designer and painted the profile of a *Princess of the House of Este* against a background of greenery scattered with flowers and butterflies.

Italy, then, had abandoned the symbolism inherited from Byzantium and tried to represent the visible world according to a rational conception. About 1420, Masaccio, a brilliant innovator, infused fresh vigour into Florentine art by a quite new kind of realism. He glorified man, who was now seen objectively in relation to the world around him. He absorbed the latest

31

Sandro Botticelli.
1444/45-1510.
Fresco
from the Villa Lemmi.
Detail.   About 1484.

ideas of the sculptors and gave solidity and poise to his figures
and their clothes. The play of shadows and the tonal values of
light over receding planes created a homogeneous atmosphere.
The rational Florentines explored the world of outer appearances
with their scientific speculation and perspective was invented.
Paolo Uccello was fascinated by these learned experiments,
which interfered with his sleep and, consequently, his wife's
as well.   In the *Rout of San Romano*, Uccello applied with
determination and evident satisfaction the laws of foreshor-
tening to the drawing of the horses. Several combattants wear
the big Tuscan head-gear, the *mazzocchio*, whose shape
required a particularly delicate draughtsmanship.   A monk
called Guido di Pietro, better known by the nickname earned
him by the purity of his art, Fra Angelico, combined a strong
Christian faith with the first attempts of modern art to master
the structure of space and create a rational representation of

LÉONARD DE VINCI. 1452-1519. LA VIERGE ET L'ENFANT AVEC SAINTE ANNE. VERS 1506/10
LEONARDO DA VINCI. VIRGIN AND CHILD WITH ST ANNE. ABOUT 1506/10.
LEONARDO DA VINCI. DIE HEILIGE ANNA SELBDRITT. UM 1506/10
LEONARDO DE VINCI. 1452-1519. LA VIRGEN Y EL NINO CON SANTA ANA. HACIA 1506/10
LEONARDO DA VINCI. 1452-1519. LA VERGINE E IL BAMBINO CON SANT'ANNA. VERSO 1506/10

Raphael.
1483-1520.
La Belle Jardinière.
1507.

Raphael.
Baldassare Castiglione.
About 1514.

33

Giorgione. 1478?-1510. Le Concert Champêtre.

the world. The symmetrically grouped saints in his *Coronation of the Virgin* are united in a common joy. In this paradise flooded with light, all the colours of the rainbow adorn the robes of the blessed. Although a miracle of art suggests their three-dimensional qualities, the figures are unencumbered by any bodily weight. In Angelico's old age, Gozzoli became his assistant (*Triumph of St Thomas Aquinas*) and described the Tuscan landscape and architecture with a miniaturist's detail.

In the second half of the 15th century, humanism opened new paths for Italian painting. Artists were enthralled by the beauty of their classical heritage and tried to reconcile its spiritual values with those of Christianity. Cultivated patrons commissioned them to illustrate the ancient stories and commented on their moral significance.

Painting was particularly receptive to these new tendencies; the idealised images of Andrea Mantegna at Mantua (*Parnassus*) and Botticelli at Florence gave expression to the new culture, while their religious compositions, in contrast, reflect their tormented faith. Mantegna copied classical costumes and buildings with archaeological fidelity (*St Sebastian; Calvary*).

34

Titian.
About 1485-1576.
Young Woman
at her Toilet.
About 1512-1515.

Titian.
Man with a Glove.
About 1520.

35

Tintoretto. 1518-1594. Susanna and the Elders.

The firm, supple draughtsmanship of the Florentines is a reminder that they often served their apprenticeship with a goldsmith. Botticelli is one of the most attractive of them because of his colouring, which is so fresh with its harmonious greens and rose in the *Frescoes of the Villa Lemmi*. Baldovinetti shows the same sensitive refinement in the way he bathes the Madonna's face with a silvery chiaroscuro in his *Virgin and Child* and stretches a wooded, hilly landscape behind her; his grace and mystery anticipate Leonardo da Vinci. Ghirlandaio was not only a generous and skilled decorator, but also a great portraitist (*An old Man and his Grandson*). Michelangelo was one of his pupils, while the young Raphael studied under the Umbrian Perugino (*St Sebastian*).

Like Michelangelo, who is represented in the Louvre by sculpture, Leonardo da Vinci is one of the masters in whom the contrasting currents of Florence met; he is the culmination of nearly a century of effort. Painting for him was the highest activity of the mind (*cosa mentale*) and required a universal knowledge. His technique of gently shadowed modelling

Veronese. 1528-1588. Calvary. About 1570.

(*sfumato*) gave his faces an imperceptible smile, veiling the soul in an unknown retreat, a symbol of the human mystery; it gave a subdued shimmer to the countryside, grottoes and mountaintops, a symbol of the mysteries of nature that haunted the investigations of this universal scholar (*Virgin of the Rocks; Virgin and St Anne;* Mona Lisa Gherardini, wife of Francesco Zanobi del Giocondo, the legendary *Gioconda*). Leonardo painted in Milano where Boltraffio followed his example (*Virgin of the Casio Family*). Marco d'Oggiono's copy gives the visitor to the Louvre an idea of Leonardo's *Last Supper* at Milan.

Half way along the Grande Galerie, a gentleman keeps respectful company with the Mona Lisa. It is *Baldassare Castiglione*, painted by his friend, Raphael. It is the Castiglione who described in the treatise, *The Courtier*, his conceptions of moral elegance which also comprise the aesthetic of Italian classicism. It required nobility of human beings and placed the creative act of the artist under the sign of love, the guiding principle of knowledge and beauty. This ideal was embodied in

37

Caravaggio.   1573-1610.   The Fortune-teller.   About 1590.

Raphael, who was painting at Florence in 1505, then at Rome under the pontificates of Julius II and Leo X (*Holy Family* of Francis I; *La Belle Jardinière*). Florence then received a reflection from the High Renaissance at Rome to which she had con-

Guardi.   1712-1793.   The Doge embarking on the Bucentaur.

tributed (Andrea del Sarto: *Charity*). At Parma, the voluptuous and erotic art of Correggio (*Antiope; Mystic Marriage of St Catherine*) takes us to Venice.

In her slightly isolated position in the peninsula, Venice had travelled along the road that led from Byzantine archaism (Paolo Veneziano: *Virgin* against a gold background) to the pre-classical art of Giovanni Bellini and Antonello da Messina (*Condottiere*). The republic's connections with the eastern

PHOTO GIRAUDON

Canaletto. 1697-1768. The Grand Canal and Santa Maria della Salute.

world is reflected in Carpaccio's *St Stephen Preaching*, which is set in a Jerusalem bristling with Muslim minarets, and Gentile Bellini went to Constantinople. His half-brother, Giovanni Bellini (*Portrait of a Man*) trained about thirty painters, one of whom was Giorgione, the Venetian Leonardo. Giorgione, in his too brief existence, was a lover, a page who played the lute divinely, and was fêted by the gilded youth of Venice. He was an early romantic and one of the creators of the modern mind. His *Concert Champêtre* is set among the wooded hills of Asolo at the close of the day; it seems as if the flow of time has stopped. He introduced music, love, nature, dreaming and silence into painting. Titian, with a more intense voluptuousness,

39

School of Avignon.   Pietà.   About 1460.

orchestrated these themes into a powerful whole and indued women with an almost mystical dignity (*Venus of the Pardo*). The model of *Young Woman at her Toilet* was the favourite of a prince. Whether she was Laura de Dianti or Isabella Boschetti is a rather indiscreet question.   However, the model of the *Virgin with a Rabbit* and the melancholy young woman of the *Allegory* are none other than the artist's wife, Cecilia.   His contemporaries, Palma Vecchio, Sebastiano del Piombo and Bonifacio de' Pitati, associated the most moving and evocative aspects of nature with the image of woman in her most voluptuous beauty.   Veronese offered Venice a picture of its pomps and triumphs; Charles V and the Grand Turk, Suleiman, are seated with Christ among the guests of the *Wedding at Cana;* the four greatest painters of Venice living in 1560 play instruments in the orchestra: old Titian the bass, Veronese and Tintoretto the viols, Bassano da Ponte the reed pipe. Veronese was a worldly painter, but in a contemplative moment he painted the little *Crucifixion*, like Tintoretto, who conceived one of the grandest visions of *Paradise;* the Louvre possesses the preliminary study for the vast painting in the Palazzo Ducale at Venice.   Bassano da Ponte's realism was often of a popular kind (*Deposition from the Cross*) and anticipated Caravaggio's,

Jean Fouquet.
1420? 1480?.
Charles VII,
King of France.
1444-1445.

Master
of Moulins.
St Mary
Magdalen with
a Donor.
About 1490-1495.

41

François Clouet.
About 1520-1572.
Elizabeth
of Austria.
1571.

School of
Fontainebleau.
Diana the Huntress.
About 1550-1600.

Louis Le Nain. About 1593-1648. Peasant family in an Interior. About 1643.

one of the greatest painters of the 17th century (*Death of the Virgin*). The Genoese Castigliono, the Roman Domenico Feti, Luca Giordano at Naples and Guercino at Bologna, one after another used the effects of his dramatic chiaroscuro. The Venetian Piazzetta painted the glittering enchantment of the baroque and Venice possesses in Tiepolo the greatest European decorative painter of the 18th century (*Last Supper*). Canaletto and Guardi recorded the civic ceremonies of Venice and the reflection of her marble palaces in the green waters of the lagoon.

France. French art, which is so rich in tapestry and sculpture, made an impressive beginning in painting during the 14th and 15th centuries. The upheavals of the Hundred Years War and later the Wars of Religion prevented France, until the middle of the 17th century, from producing painting with the wealth and continuity that are the glory of Flanders and Italy. The influence of these two great centres of culture was felt for a long time from the two towns that were most affected by it: Avignon, where the popes encouraged Sienese painting during their stay; and Dijon, the capital of a Franco-Flemish duchy. The centres at Paris and Val de Loire complete the picture of pictorial activity in France during the 15th century. When the Great Schism ended, the artistic activity of the Provençal centre produced work with a purely French flavour. A

43

PHOTO GIRAUDON

Philippe de
Champaigne.
1602-1674.
Ex-voto of 1662.

Baugin.
The Five Senses.

PHOTO GIRAUDON

dignified emotion emanates from the *Pietà* of Villeneuve-lès-
Avignon; it is still medieval in its hieratic use of a gold background, modern in the realistic portrait of the donor, French in
the silent expression of grief. Equally poignant is the large,
round *Pietà*, in which the influence of Siena seems stronger
than that of Bruges, in spite of the Flemish origin of Jean
Malouel to whom it is attributed. The subject (*Last Commu-*

GEORGES DE LA TOUR. 1593-1652. LA MADELEINE A LA VEILLEUSE. VERS 1630/35
GEORGES DE LA TOUR. MARY MAGDALEN WITH A NIGHT-LIGHT
GEORGES DE LA TOUR. DIE HEILIGE MAGDALENA MIT.LAMPE. UM 1630/35
GEORGES DE LA TOUR. 1593-1652. LA MAGDALENA DEL CANDIL. HACIA 1630/35
GEORGES DE LA TOUR. 1593-1652. LA MADDALENA COL LUME. VERSO 1630/35

Nicolas Poussin, 1594 1665. Shepherds in Arcadia. About 1638.

nion and Martyrdom of St Denys) of several paintings, their destination (*Altar-piece of the Parliament of Paris*), or views of the city's buildings (*Pietà of Saint Germain-des-Prés*) connect them with the centre at Paris. Others are unmistakably Parisian by their style; although the Master of the Altar-frontal of Narbonne borrowed his group of holy women at the foot of the cross from Siena, the elegance of his gothic draperies and precise draughtsmanship belong to the Parisian miniaturists whom Dante praised at the end of the 13th century. The beginnings and first outstanding examples of French portraiture appeared at the Valois court with the profile portrait of the red-haired, sly-looking *Jean le Bon*, still marked by Giotto's style, and the three-quarter face portraits painted by Jean Fouquet, a native of Val de Loire and the greatest French master of the 15th century. He had studied Italian architecture and the spatial values of the Florentines. The masterly technique and psychological insight of his portraits are as admirable now as they were in his own day (*Charles VII; Guillaume Juvénal des Ursins*). Towards the end of the century, when the tormented style of late gothic was on the decline in France, the gentleness and ample modelling of the Master of Moulins' portraits (*Child Praying; St Magdalen with a Donor*) have much in common with the placid art of Memlinc and Perugino.

45

Claude Lorrain. 1600-1682. Seaport at Sunset. About 1639.

Charles VIII and Francis I both admired Italy and naturally attracted Italian artists to France. The Florentine Rosso, Primaticcio (*Diana the Huntress*) and Niccolò dell'Abbate (*Abduction of Proserpina*), both from Bologna, came to decorate Fontainebleau. They brought mannerism with them, a refined product of the Italian courts after the death of Raphael. They deliberately elongated the human form, which gave it the unhealthy gracility so cherished by the court of Henri II. This was the early School of Fontainebleau. Later, François Clouet and Jean Cousin the Elder (*Eva prima Pandora*) worked together to create an aristocratic art whose principal themes were women, hunting and the forest. This second phase of the School of Fontainebleau (*Gabrielle d'Estrées and the Duchesse de Villars*), like the contemporary love poetry, is burdened with classical allusions to the life of the court that lives on in the meticulous portraits, painted or drawn, of Corneille de Lyon and the Clouets. Caron, on the fringe of the Fontainebleau School, made allusions to the first brutalities of the Wars of the Religion, under cover of Roman history (*Massacre of the Triumvirs*).

Two major currents of 17th century European painting originated in Italy. At Bologna, the Carracci, Domenichino and

46

Watteau.
1684-1721.
Gilles.

Watteau.
La Finette.

47

François Boucher. 1703-1770. Diana resting after her Bath. 1742.

Guido Reni had laid the foundations of a composite art that drew on the varied and complementary qualities of the great 16th century masters. This eclecticism had its French followers: Simon Vouet (*Presentation in the Temple*) and Lesueur (*Life of St Bruno*); the profane paintings of Blanchard (*Cimon and Iphigenia*) bore a superficial resemblance to the voluptuousness of Titian. The other current, the style of realism and chiaroscuro that Caravaggio created at Rome, had more far-reaching consequences. Art centres as far apart as Toulouse, Nancy and Utrecht were affected by it. The Le Nain brothers, natives of Laon, were familiar with the intimate life of country folk, which they painted in serious or homely scenes (*The Forge; Peasants' Meal; The Cart*), and introduced peasants into their religious compositions (*The Manger*). Children in their paintings are appealingly graceful and mischievous. This '' great age of souls '', when the Catholic revival produced a number of saints, inspired the mystical work of the great Lorrainer, Georges de La Tour. Humble people meditate by a meagre candle-light in the dark night of his religious paintings (*Adoration of the Shepherds; Mary Magdalen with a Night-light*). The Le Nain brothers, Georges de La Tour and Baugin, with the almost monastic frugality of his still-lifes (*The Five Senses*), belong

JEAN-BAPTISTE CHARDIN. 1699-1779. LE BÉNÉDICITÉ. 1740
JEAN-BAPTISTE CHARDIN. GRACE. 1740
JEAN-BAPTISTE CHARDIN. DAS TISCHGEBET. 1740.
JEAN-BAPTISTE CHARDIN. LA BENDICION DE LA MESA. 1740
JEAN-BAPTISTE CHARDIN. IL BENEDICITE. 1740

Jean-Honoré Fragonard. 1732-1806. The Bathers. 1775.

to the school of realism, as it was called in an exhibition in 1934 of the genre. The austerity of these works, which was already classical, reached its finest expression of spirituality in Philippe de Champaigne, a Fleming, who painted the inspired faces of the Jansenists. In contrast to Bolognese art, which painted the paroxysms of ecstasy, the *Ex Voto of 1662* and *Mother Catherine Agnès Arnauld with Sister Catherine of Sainte-Suzanne, daughter of the Painter* express a wholly inward serenity and faith.

Two painters, Nicolas Poussin and Claude Gellée, called Claude Lorrain, settled in Rome where they defined the ideal of French classicism in their history painting and landscapes. Claude Lorrain was one of the great poets of nature and light; in his seascapes, the disc of the sun floods the sky with its light and is reflected on the waves of the Tyrrhenian Sea. The great figures of history and legend, their palaces and squadrons liven the shore (*Ulysses restoring Chryseis to her Father; Cleopatra disembarking at Tarsus*). He sometimes recorded the ruins of Rome as they stood (*Campo Vaccino*). The southern light of his paintings is not the silvery grey that diffuses over the view of Rome from the Pincio at mid-day, but the amber-gold that floods towards the evening over the city seen from the Janiculum. Poussin and Lorrain both sketched freely during their hours of

Jacques-Louis David.   1748-1825.   Madame Récamier.   1800.

study.   In his landscapes that formed the setting for Biblical
and historical scenes (*Summer, or Ruth and Boaz*), Poussin
tamed the wildness of nature, discarded its ephemeral aspects
and arranged its elements into a preconceived design.   They
provide a solemn background to an often pessimistic comment
on the brevity of life (*Shepherds in Arcadia*), the solitude of
man, the tragedy of destiny (*Orpheus and Eurydice*) and the
vanity of worldly success (*Funeral of Phocion*).

The visitor should go to Versailles to appreciate the painting
of the autocratic reign of Louis XIV, dedicated to the glorification of royal policies and docile to the dogmatic directives of
an Academy founded by Colbert.   The skill and prolific output
of Le Brun (*The Chancellor Séguier entering Paris*) made him the
outstanding personality among a crowd of decorative painters.
He was later supplanted by old Mignard (*The Dauphin and his
Family*) who had excelled in religious decorative painting and
portraiture.   The monarchy, with its Spanish rigidity of etiquette,
employed Rigaud (*Louis XIV in Coronation Robes*) and Largil-
lière (*The Farmer-general De Laage*) for its state portraits.
The end of the century saw the outbreak of a struggle between
academicism, originating in Bologna, and the colour values of
Flemish painting.   The triumph of the Rubenists over the Pous-

Antoine-Jean Gros.
1771-1835.
Bonaparte at
the Bridge of Arcola.
1796.

Théodore Géricault.
1791-1824.
Cavalry officer
of the Imperial
Guard.
1812.

Jean-Auguste Ingres.   1780-1867.   The Turkish Bath.   1863.

sinists was the triumph of feeling over intellect. It set the inde-
pendent art of the 18th century on new paths.

Watteau came to Paris from the Flemish borderlands and
died of consumption when he was thirty-seven years old. He
was shy, secretive, musical and a little misanthropic in spite of
the large circle of friends his gentleness and genius won for
him (*L'Indifférent*).   Women and love once again became
important in French painting through him. The sensibility and
conventions of his '' fêtes galantes '' had been sharpened and
enriched from age to age in French literature and art. There is
already a suggestion of them in the 15th century illuminated
manuscripts of the *Très Riches Heures du Duc de Berry* and the
Cœur d'amour épris. The theme of the Happy Isle, taken up

52

Ingres.
Madame Panckoucke.
1811.

Théodore Chassériau.
1819-1856.
The Two Sisters.
1843.

Eugène Delacroix.   1798-1863.   Liberty leading the People.   1830.

in the *Embarkation for Cythera*, went back to the precious romanticism of Louis XIII's reign, and Louis XIV's court had glimpsed the Enchanted Isle in one of its festivities. For some people this is not the departure for the Isle of Venus, suggested by the far distant mists, but the nostalgic return of a pilgrimage to it. The unsatisfied heart of the sick longs for inaccessible lands; the figures of the *Gathering in the Park* hardly show more than their backs; time flows on without a stop and reality is unrelenting. With his consummate Flemish technique, Watteau quickens the silk of dresses and light foliage with the same shimmer. The courtly strain was slight among his followers: Lancret (*Conversation in a Park*); decorative with Boucher (*Diana resting after her Bath*); sensual and already romantic with Fragonard (*Sleeping Bacchante; The Bathers; Vow of Love*). The tone of this art suited the society which showed a decided preference for the portrait. It is impersonal under the brush of Nattier, a discreet analysis in velvety colour by Perronneau (*Madame de Sorquainville*) and naturally elegant with Mme Vigée-Le Brun (*Madame de Polignac*). The pastels of Quentin La Tour, kept in the Cabinet des Dessins, surprised

54

contemporary writers in the heat of philosophical discussions and include the charming portrait of their protector, Madame de Pompadour. Far from the frivolities of society, in a simple lodging in Saint Germain-des-Prés, Chardin leisurely developed his still-lifes and interiors. His integrity ennobled with an almost religious dignity the humblest objects (*Silver Goblet*) as well as the everyday tasks of the housewife who cared to see herself in his pictures (*The Purveyor; Grace*). In contrast, Greuze's paintings of common life were enveloped in philosophical moralising and a confused, lacrymose mawkishness (*The Village Betrothal; The Broken Pitcher*).

The European movement of baroque art, typified by the generous style of Rubens and Tiepolo ended in the 18th century with the gracious feminine forms of the rococo, whose spirit appears in the work of Watteau and the decorative painters of his day. A renewed admiration for Greco-Roman civilisation made itself felt in reaction against the tendencies of two

Eugène Delacroix. Algerian Women. 1834.

Gustave Courbet. 1819-1877. The Painter's Studio. Detail. 1855.

centuries of art. It inspired the painters of the Revolution and
the Empire. An idealist aesthetic, the impetus given to archaeo-
logy by the discovery of Herculaneum, the examples of republican virtues described by Latin historians were the sources of
David's heroic, glacial painting (*The Oath of the Horatii;
Leonidas at Thermopylae; Battle of the Romans and the
Sabines*). In his huge composition, *The Coronation of Napoleon I*, David solved the problems of etiquette and precedence
which required that no dignitary should be neglected. Napo-

56

JEAN-BAPTISTE COROT. 1796-1875. L'ÉGLISE DE MARISSEL.1866
JEAN-BAPTISTE COROT. CHURCH AT MARISSEL. 1866
JEAN-BAPTISTE COROT. DIE KIRCHE VON MARISSEL.1866.
JEAN-BAPTISTE COROT. 1796-1875. LA IGLESIA DE MARISSEL. 1866
JEAN-BAPTISTE COROT. 1796-1875. LA CHIESA DI MARISSEL. 1866

Honoré Daumier.　1808-1879.　Crispin and Scapin.　About 1860.

leon has crowned himself and is just crowning Josephine, while the pope, under obvious constraint, makes a vague gesture of benediction. The Davidian ideal was shared by Guérin (*Return of Marcus Sextus*) and Girodet (*Funeral of Atala; Endymion Sleeping*), but soon a conflict is noticeable between the taste for an icy perfection and the desire for a freer, more colourful art, springing from the heart and the imaginative power that romanticism was to liberate. This clash between official doctrine and their deepest aspirations brought failure to Girodet (*The Flood*) and led Baron Gros to suicide. Correggio's vibrant light glanced over the pearly flesh of Prud'hon's nymphs (*Psyche borne away by the Zephyrs*). Gros, who recorded the wars of the Empire and whom Napoleon preferred to David, made effective use of colour, light and movement. He was already a romantic when he painted *Christine Boyer*, the portrait of a young woman. He exalted his hero (*Bonaparte at the Bridge of Arcola*), was interested in the east (*The Plague-stricken of Jaffa*) and, in the midst of the dead strewn over the snowy plain of Eylau, painted the victor as a sad, human figure. Géricault, a dandy passionately fond of riding, paid homage to the horsemen of the imperial army (*Cavalry officer of the Imperial Guard*), then he studied the insane (*The Mad Woman*), executed criminals and corpses.

Jan van Eyck. About 1390-1441 ?. Madonna with the Chancellor Rolin. About 1435.

He recorded the appalling incident of the *Raft of the Medusa* at the moment most fraught with human significance, when the dying saw a chance of being saved.

One of David's pupils was a young man from Montauban, Ingres, who was to become the greatest draughtsman of the French School. His interest in Greek vases, the Quattrocento and Raphael, the Middle Ages of the troubadours and Persian miniatures was reflected in what Baudelaire called his " heteroclite " art. Whenever Ingres sacrificed to Greco-Roman classicism, his painting is intolerably boring (*Apotheosis of Homer*). Like his great rival, Delacroix, and his pupil, Chassériau (*Toilet of Esther*), he was attracted to the east (*Odalisque; The Bather*). His *Turkish Bath* was bought by an Ottoman diplomat. He

Roger van der Weyden. 1399?-1464. Annunciation.

was a painter of the small, isolated subject rather than large, complex scenes. His sensitiveness to feminine beauty and exceptionally refined draughtsmanship can be appreciated in the portraits with their undulating arabesques and penetrating charm (*Madame Rivière*).

Ingres has been described as classic in contrast to Delacroix, who is bracketed with Hugo and Berlioz to make the trinity of French romanticism. In fact, Delacroix grasped the essence of life and movement, and used colour with the emotive power the Venetians taught him. His paintings in the Louvre justify Taine's judgment: '' He went everywhere in search of human tragedy at its greatest, in Byron, Dante, Tasso, Shakespeare, in the east and Greece, around us and in dreams and

Hans Memlinc.
1433?-1494.
Mystic Marriage
of Saint Catherine.

history. '' He borrowed from Byron *Don Juan's Shipwreck*, and *Dante and Virgil in the Infernal Regions* from Dante, who recognised Florentines whom he knew among the damned. Shakespeare provided him with *Hamlet and Horatio in the Cemetery* and the *Death of Ophelia*. *Women of Algiers* shows his fascination for the secret life of these women's quarters. From the east came the *Death of Sardanapalus*, where the king is ordering the massacre of his household; odalisques struggle under the daggers of eunuchs and horses rear at the smell of death. In the *Massacre at Chios*, where he painted the sufferings of the palikars, a dead woman and her living baby, he shows his

Lucas
van Leyden.
About
1494-1533.
Lot with
his Daughters.

sympathy for the misfortunes of the Greeks in his own day. 1830 offered him an epic theme, *Liberty leading the People*, where the goddess appears among the Gavroches, workers and bourgeois. Later on, the realistic and plebeian Courbet (*The Painter's Studio; Burial at Ornans*) said: " Goddesses! you want me to paint them... well, show me some. "

A love of nature, the deep spring of romanticism, had liberated landscape. It was sometimes tragic and desolate (Georges Michel), more often melancholy and contemplative (Théodore Rousseau and the Barbizon School) and Corot (*Chartres Cathedral; Belfry at Douai; Memory of Mortefontaine*),

Frans Hals.
1580/81-1666.
The Gipsy.
1625/28.

who for forty years had refined his soft tones and silver greys, gave it a subtle distinction. He went three times to Italy in the steps of Poussin and Claude Lorrain (*Bridge at Narni*). Yet, France owes her most telling portraits to him.

Flemish and Dutch Schools. At the end of the 14th century and during the first years of the 15th, all the schools of western painting seem moved by a common spirit. A wave of mysticism and the last flowering of chivalrous culture in the courts of the north were the formative forces of this international art of which the Limbourg brothers, some masters of the upper Rhineland, Stefano da Verona and Pisanello represent various tendencies. They all communicate a wondering vision of creation. The naturalistic current from this source flowed in different directions in the Netherlands and Germanic countries, but it is still possible to distinguish, from one stage to the next, certain characteristics common to every centre and to recognise the unity of the European renaissance.

Jan van Eyck's *Madonna with the Chancellor Rolin* sets the religious scene in an interior with a spacious view onto a

Rembrandt
van Rijn.
1606-1669.
Portrait of
the Artist
at his Easel.
1660.

PHOTO S GIRAUDON

Rembrandt.
Hendrickje
Stoffels.
1652.

PHOTO GIRAUDON

Rembrandt.　Bathsheba.　1654.

landscape.　Interior and landscape: these two genres largely
accounted for the efforts of Dutch painting until its decline.
Van Eyck was the first outstanding figure of Flemish painting
and occupies a place in northern art comparable to Masaccio's
in Italy.　He taught his countrymen scrupulous objectivity in
portraiture and a perspective where colour values gradually
faded with distance.　He is credited with the invention of oil
painting which enabled him to give a shimmer to sumptuous
tissues and the atmosphere of remote views.　The use of oil was

JOHANNES VERMEER. 1632-1675. LA DENTELLIÈRE. VERS 1664
JAN VERMEER. THE LACE-MAKER. ABOUT 1664
JAN VERMEER. DIE SPITZENKLÖPPLERIN. UM 1664
JUAN VERMEER. 1632-1675. LA ENCAJERA. HACIA 1664
JOHANNES VERMEER. 1632-1675. LA MERLETTAIA. VERSO 1664

Jacob van Ruisdael. 1628-1682. The Sunburst. 1670/75.

Willem Claesz Heda. 1594-1680. Still life with Dessert. 1637.

PHOTO GIRAUDON

Quentin Metsys. 1465-1530. The Moneylender and his Wife. 1514

a strong encouragement to the progress of realism. In the work of Roger van der Weyden (*Braque Family Triptych: the Annunciation*) and Dieric Bouts (*Deposition from the Cross*), Van Eyck's serenity disappeared before an emotional tension which is again noticeable among the artists of Ferrara where Roger van der Weyden worked. At the end of the century, this was slightly eased with the attractive mysticism of Memlinc (*Jacques Floreins and his Family presented to the Virgin*) and his pupil, Gerard David. The art of these two contemporaries of Bellini and Perugino was in keeping with the devotion of the Beguines and the placid optimism of the Bruges burghers. After them, the Flemish 16th century opened with the decline of Bruges and the rise of Antwerp, where the art of Jan Gossaert, better known as Mabuse, and Bernard van Orley developed under the influence of Italian classicism, but Flemish landscape continued on its original path. The perspective of the Netherlanders ignored the central vanishing point that controlled the vision of the Italians. By focussing the visual rays over an extended view, it included every part of landscape.

Pieter Bruegel, the Elder.   About 1525-1569.   The Beggars.   1568.

Patinir (*St Jerome in the Desert*) sweeps nature with a gigantic glance and concentrates its infinite aspects in one minute painting.   There was a satiric vein running through Pieter Bruegel I's genius as a landscapist, which was shared by the surrealistic Jerome Bosch (*Ship of Fools*) and Lucas van Leyden: *Lot with his Daughters* before Sodom struck with fire from heaven.

The unity of the Low Countries was broken in the 17th century.   While the Flemish provinces and Catholic south remained under Austrian domination, the north amalgamated into the democratic and Protestant state that was to become Holland. In Flanders, Rubens made Antwerp one of the artistic capitals of Europe.   He poured into his innumerable compositions the ebullient energy that ranks his work among the greatest painting.   Twenty-one paintings, formerly at the Luxembourg, record the life and rather inglorious regency of Marie de'Medici. In spite of the tepid enthusiasm he felt for her politics, Rubens succeeded with a few nudes, like the group of the *Three Graces*, and the realistic portraits of people.   Henry IV, glancing side-

Jan Gossaert, called Mabuse.   About 1478-1533/36.   The Carondelet Diptych.

ways at the portrait of a young princess presented by Cupid, is a masterpiece of retrospective humour. " All the women he painted, " wrote Fromentin, " seem to have contracted, in spite of themselves and in spite of him, a curious air of the already known from their contact with persisting memories. " Are we to believe that he was thinking of his first wife, Isabella Brandt, while he was painting the second, *Helena Fourment*, surrounded with her delightful children? In the *Village Fair*, Rubens painted without a trace of vulgarity the exuberant gaiety of the merry-makers, one of the inexhaustible themes of Flemish realism. Van Dyck was a product of his school. The aristocratic nonchalance of his portraits was much appreciated at Genoa and in England (*Charles I of England*). There is a hackneyed flavour about Jordaens' religious painting, in the manner of Caravaggio (*The Four Evangelists*).

Calvinist and republican Holland offered its painters neither churches nor palaces to decorate. They were limited to the narrow resources of realism and reproduced with admirable faithfulness the outward appearances of people and objects. The merchant society of Haarlem and Amsterdam recognised itself in the dignified austerity of their portraits (Verspronck and

PIERRE-PAUL RUBENS. 1577-1640. HÉLÈNE FOURMENT ET DEUX DE SES ENFANTS.
VERS 1636
PETER-PAUL RUBENS. HELENA FOURMENT WITH TWO OF HER CHILDREN. ABOUT 1636
PETER-PAUL RUBENS. HELENE FOURMENT MIT ZWEI IHRER KINDER. UM 1636
PEDRO-PABLO RUBENS. 1577-1640. ELENA FOURMENT Y DOS DE SUS HIJOS. HACIA 1636
PIETRO-PAOLO RUBENS. 1577-1640. ELENA FOURMENT E DUE DEI SUOI FIGLI. VERSO 1636

Jacob Jordaens. 1593-1678. The Four Evangelists.

Thomas de Keyser). Numerous confraternities, which were
an indication of the social cohesion that was the strength of
this little country's political success, commisioned group portraits (Van der Helst), but only Rembrandt's genius and Hals'
free technique (*The Gipsy*) could produce masterpieces in this
difficult genre. Scenes of bourgeois life, the order and tidiness
of Dutch houses inspired the intimism of Terborch and Pieter
de Hooch. Under the soft and limpid light penetrating these
interiors, a magic surrounds with its silence and serenity the
figures painted by Vermeer (*Lace-maker*). One of the greatest
of all painters, he died leaving his paintings in pawn at his

baker's and his work remained unknown until the 19th century. Something of his peaceful intimacy lay over the still-life and the motionless silence of these piles of Flemish meat, fish and vegetables. The style of the genre in Flanders was more subdued, sometimes precious, always recollected, in the penumbra of chiaroscuro (Willem Claesz Heda). A play of

Anthony van Dyck. 1599-1641. Charles I, King of England. 1635.

Albrecht Dürer
1471-1528.
Self-portrait.
1493.

PHOTO GIRAUDON

light from Caravaggio's painting shines over Honthorst's joyful
gatherings (*The Concert*) while the landscapists were loving
interpreters of the limpid marine light of the Zuyder Zee.
They were sensitive, contemplative artists who excelled in
painting great, cloudy skies, sunny glades and plains, mists
and unruffled water (Jacob van Ruisdael: *Sunburst;* Hobbema:
Water-mill; Van Goyen).   One painter, who was almost self-
taught, Rembrandt, stands outside the development of the
Dutch School and takes his place among the leading artists of
all time. The most moving of his paintings in the Louvre belong
to his maturity during a period, when he no longer tried to
please the exacting tastes of his fellow-countrymen and had
got over his financial worries, legal troubles, puritanical perse-
cution and solitude. He painted innumerable portraits of himself (*Rembrandt in old Age*) and his family. Hendrickje Stoffels
was the companion of his difficult times as Saskia had shared
his success. That masterpiece inspired by affection, the portrait of Hendrickje, the servant metamorphosed into a princess,

71

Lucas Cranach,
the Elder.
1472-1553.
Venus.

is probably, of all the Louvre paintings, the one that prompts
the innermost questioning of the soul's secrets. The same
woman may have inspired the pensive and rather heavy
Bathsheba in which X-ray photographs have revealed three
pentimenti in the position of the head. Rembrandt was brought
up on the Bible. He relived the Old and New Testaments through
his Jewish friendships in Amsterdam and saw in the continuity
of the oriental tradition the first witness of the word of love
(*The Good Samaritan*). The secret of the intense effulgence
in the *Pilgrims at Emmaus* lies in the humbleness of the setting,
the figures and the art itself, which reduce the revelation of the
divine presence to a taut interplay of lines and colours.

LUCAS CRANACH. 1472-1553. PORTRAIT DE FILLETTE
LUCAS CRANACH. PORTRAIT OF A YOUNG GIRL
LUCAS CRANACH. BILDNIS EINES JUNGEN MÄDCHENS
LUCAS CRANACH. 1472. RETRATO DE MUCHACHA
LUCAS CRANACH. 1472. RITRATTO DI FANCIULLA

Hans Holbein.
1497/98-1543.
Anne of Cleves.
1539/40.

Hans Holbein.
Niklaus
Kratzer.
1528.

73

Hans Holbein.   Erasmus.   1523/24.

Spanish, German and English Schools.   Italy,
France and the Netherlands comprised what were called in the
18th century '' the three schools '', which were represented in
every private collections and formed the basis of the royal collections too.   Spain was sometimes considered an artistic
dependency of Italy.   The Germanic world and England were
hardly represented at all in the French collections.   The 19th
century attempted to fill these gaps without, however, succeed-
ing in acquiring very extensive holdings of these schools.
Spain had some original painters in the three centuries that
linked the Catalan primitives with Goya.   Her civilisation reached
its apogee in the late 16th century under Philip II.   The king
collected Jerome Bosch and Patinir, but misunderstood the

El Greco
(Domenikos Theotocopoulis).
1541-1614.
Christ on the Cross
and two Donors.
About 1580.

Francisco de Zurbarán.
1598-1664.
Saint Apollonia.

genius of El Greco, the Cretan, familiar with Venetian art who settled at Toledo. A tragic sky, suggested by the violent Castilian storms, gives universality to the drama of the *Crucifixion*. El Greco took the elongated human form from Italian mannerism and his figures (*Antonio Covarrubias*) evoke the soaring of prayer or the '' flame of love '' that consumed St John of the Cross. After him, the painting of mystic Spain assumed a monastic austerity in Zurbaran (*Death of St Bonaventure*) and became more sentimental and realistic with Murillo (*The Angels' Kitchen*). Ribera showed his pity for the proud poverty of the Spanish people (*The Clubfoot*) at the same time that Velazquez, who was deeply interested in ordinary life himself was immortalising the court of Philip IV (*The Infanta Marga-*

José de Ribera.
1591-1652.
The Clubfoot.
1652.

Bartolomé
Estebán Murillo.
1618-1682.
Young Beggar.
1645/55.

rita; Queen Mariana). A last, solitary genius appeared on the
eve of romanticism, Goya. The fantastic side of his art is best
known but in the Louvre he is represented by portraits, characterised by their refined colouring; *Marquésa de Solana*,
one of his masterpieces, and *Woman with a Fan*.

A Self-portrait by Albrecht Dürer is dated 1493. The artist
is holding a thistle, the symbol of conjugal fidelity, and he may
have intended this panel for his fiancée, Agnes Frey. Gœthe

VELASQUEZ. 1599-1660. PORTRAIT DE L'INFANTE MARGUERITE. VERS 1655
VELAZQUEZ. THE INFANTA MARGARITA. ABOUT 1655
VELASQUEZ. BILDNIS DER INFANTIN MARGHERITA. UM 1655
VELAZQUEZ. 1599-1660. RETRATO DE LA INFANTA MARGARITA HACIA 1655
VELASQUEZ. 1599-1660. RITRATTO DELL'INFANTE MARGHERITA. VERSO 1655

Francisco de Goya y Lucientes. 1746-1828. Marquésa de la Solana. About 1792.

Thomas Lawrence.
1769-1830.
Julius
Angerstein
and his Wife.
1792.

PHOTO E GIRAUDON

Joshua Reynolds.
1723-1792.
Master Hare.
1788/89.

knew the work from an cold copy and thought it peerless.
Around the leader of the German School are grouped Cranach
the Elder (*Venus*) and Hans Holbein the Younger, court painter
to Henry VIII of England, who portrayed his wives (*Anne of
Cleves*) and his courtiers.

England later on welcomed Van Dyck. Her greatest portrai-
tists appeared in the 18th century (Reynolds: *Master Hare*).
During the romantic period, Constable, Bonington (*Parterre
d'Eau at Versailles*), then Turner (*Sea at Margate*) treated
landscape with a technical freedom and freshness that fascinated Delacroix, Paul Huet and the Barbizon School.

Richard Parkes Bonington. 1802-1828. The Parterre d'Eau at Versailles. 1826.

John Constable. 1776-1837. Weymouth Bay. 1827.

79

Achevé d'imprimer
sur les presses de l'Imprimerie Mussot, Paris.